MAY I QUOTE YOU, GENERAL LEE?

MAY I QUOTE YOU, GENERAL LEE?

Observations & Utterances From The South's Great Generals

Two Best-selling Works Complete in One Volume

EDITED BY RANDALL BEDWELL

GRAMERCY BOOKS
NEW YORK

Contents originally published in two volumes:
    May I Quote You, General Lee? copyright © 1997 by Randall Bedwell
    May I Quote You, General Lee? Volume 2 copyright © 1998 by Randall Bedwell

This 2002 edition is published by Gramercy Books, an imprint of Random House Value
Publishing, a division of Random House, Inc., New York, by arrangement with
Cumberland House Publishing, Inc., Nashville, Tennessee.

Gramercy is a registered trademark and the colophon is a trademark of Random House, Inc.

Previously published as: *May I Quote You, General Lee?* and *May I Quote You, General
Lee? Volume 2*

Printed in the United States of America

Random House
New York • Toronto • London • Sydney • Auckland
www.randomhouse.com

Library of Congress Cataloging-in-Publication Data

May I quote you, General Lee? : observations and utterances from the South's great
generals / edited by Randall Bedwell.
        p. cm.
    Originally published: Memphis, Tenn. : Guild Bindery Press, 1995.
    ISBN 0-517-21992-1
1. Lee, Robert E. (Robert Edward), 1807–1870—Quotations. 2. United
States—History—Civil War, 1861–1865—Quotations, maxims, etc. 3. Quotations,
American. I. Bedwell, Randall J.

    E467.1.L4 M46 2002
    973.7'092—dc21

                                                                2001054300

9 8 7 6 5 4 3 2

Contents

MAY I QUOTE YOU, GENERAL LEE?

Volume One

To my grandmother,
Rebecca Hartsfield Claxton

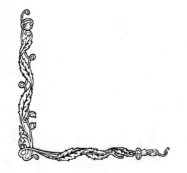

Table of Contents

Introduction

Perhaps it is the perennial appeal of the underdog that enables these gray ghosts to maintain their hold on our imaginations. While they defended their way of life with conviction (but not without reluctance), in many of these statements they reveal themselves to be mere overwhelmed individuals, and understandably so. All their actions take place in a climate of national desperation unequalled at any other time in American history save for the Revolution. In 1861, the future Confederate commanders had every reason to believe that they would be hanged should secession fail. Lives, fortunes, sacred honor: Those were the terms in which the South's wartime leaders pledged their sacrifice.

Randall J. Bedwell
Cordova, Tennessee
October 1, 1995

General Robert E. Lee

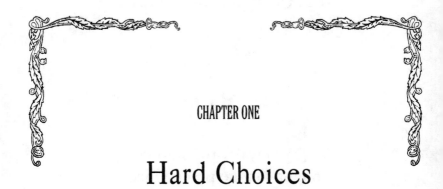

CHAPTER ONE

Hard Choices

During the bleak interlude between Lincoln's election and the eventual commencement of hostilities, almost every future Confederate commander left some written account of his arduous decision to forsake the Union. Reneging on an oath was a grave matter, and early in their careers most of these fighting men had pledged their lives to defend the Union and the Constitution that binds it. Conspicuously absent from their remarks is any enthusiasm for a military solution to the secession crisis. With solemn tones they delineate their reasons: duty, honor, principle.

✯ ✯ ✯

My loyalty to Virginia ought to take precedence over that which is due to the federal government. If Virginia stands by the old Union, so will I. But, if she secedes, then I will still follow my native state with my sword, and need be with my life.

—*Robert E. Lee to Charles Anderson,*
February 1861

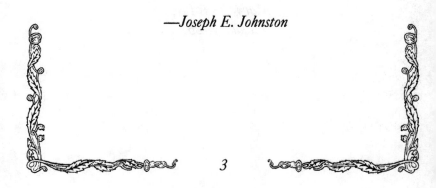

I owe all that I
am to the government
of the United States. It has
educated and clothed me with
honor. To leave the service is a hard
necessity, but I must go. Though I am
resigning my position, I trust I may
never draw my sword against
the old flag.

—*Joseph E. Johnston*

There is no sacrifice I am not ready to make for the preservation of the Union save that of honor.

—*Robert E. Lee to his wife,*
Mary Custis Lee,
January 1861

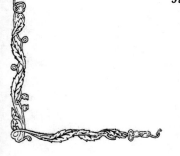
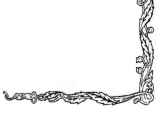

Our present political system has been achieved in a manner unprecedented in the history of nations. . . . It illustrates the American idea that governments rest on the consent of the governed, and that it is the right of the people to alter or abolish them at will whenever they become destructive of the ends for which they were established. Obstacles may retard, but they can not long prevent the progress of a movement sanctified by its justice and sustained by a virtuous people.

—President Jefferson Davis's inaugural address, Montgomery, Alabama, February 1861

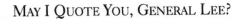

I take great
pride in my country, her
prosperity and institutions,
and would defend any state if
her rights were invaded. But I can
anticipate no greater calamity for the
country than the dissolution of the Union.
It would be an accumulation of all the
evils we complain of, and I am
willing to sacrifice everything but honor for its
preservation.

—*Robert E. Lee*

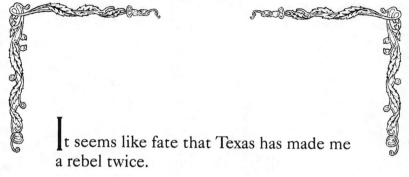

It seems like fate that Texas has made me a rebel twice.

—Albert Sidney Johnston, referring to his participation in the War for Texas Independence from Mexico

People who are anxious to bring on war don't know what they are bargaining for; they don't see all the horrors that must accompany such an event.

—Stonewall Jackson

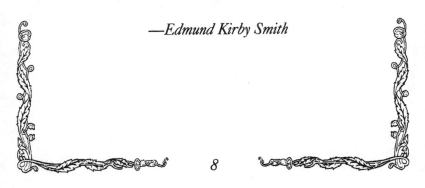

I have broken
all ties that bind me to
the [U.S.] Army, not suddenly,
impulsively, but conscientiously and
after due deliberation. I sacrifice more
to my principles than any other officer
in the Army can do. I would rather
carry a musket in the cause of the
South than be commander-in-
chief under Mr. Lincoln.

—*Edmund Kirby Smith*

The line of duty
is clear. Each one to
follow his own state if
his state goes to war; if
not, he may remain and
help on the work
of reunion.

—*Matthew Fontaine Maury*

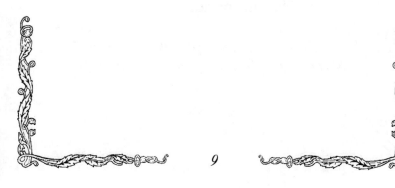

I must side either
with or against my section or
country. I cannot raise my hand
against my birthplace, my home,
my children. I should like, above all
things, that our difficulties might be
peaceably arranged. . . . Whatever may
be the result of the contest, I foresee
that the country will have to pass
through a terrible ordeal, a necessary expiation perhaps
for our national sins.

—Robert E. Lee, excerpt from a letter to a
Northern girl who had requested his photograph

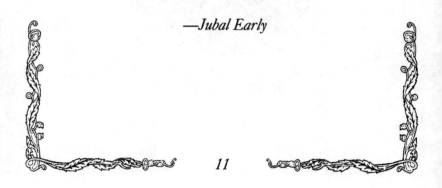

As we are now
engaged in this contest,
all my wishes, all my desires
and all the energies of my hand
and heart will be given to the cause
of my state. Whether we have the
right of secession or revolution, I
want to see my state
triumphant.

—*Jubal Early*

James Longstreet

CHAPTER TWO

Fighting Words

With the fate of nations hanging in the balance, little wonder that things said under the stress of battle often seem masterpieces of understatement. Though hostile circumstances dictated brevity, the power of such statements lies in their pith, and the history of warfare is replete with examples of such stirring words. The heightened adrenalin-induced awareness brought about by combat—what Winston Churchill called the "exhilaration" of being shot at and missed—loosens poetry in men. What they say sometimes means the difference between victory and defeat.

There is Jackson standing like a stone wall. Let us determine to die here, and we will conquer.

—*General Barnard E. Bee describing Thomas J. "Stonewall" Jackson's brigade at First Bull Run, 1861*

You have your bayonets!

—*Thomas C. Hindman's response to a subordinate who advised against mounting a charge due to a lack of ammunition, Shiloh, 1862*

Major, send a shell first over their heads and let them get in their holes before you open with all your guns.

—*John Bell Hood, advancing up the Rappahannock, 1863*

We shall attack at daylight tomorrow. I would fight them if they were a million.

—*Albert Sidney Johnston, Shiloh, 1862*

Form platoons! Draw saber! Charge!

—*J.E.B. Stuart's standard cavalry order*

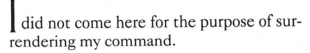

I did not come here for the purpose of surrendering my command.

> —*Nathan Bedford Forrest, Fort Donelson, 1862*

Tonight we will water our horses in the Tennessee River.

> —*Albert Sidney Johnston, Shiloh, 1862*

General Lee: How many men will you take?

General Jackson: My whole corps.

General Lee: Well, go on.

> —*Last words exchanged between Robert E. Lee and Stonewall Jackson, Chancellorsville, 1863. It was decided there to risk dividing the Confederate force in a bold flanking march to turn Hooker's right.*

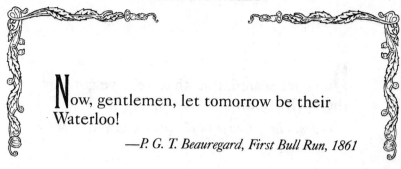

Now, gentlemen, let tomorrow be their
Waterloo!

—P. G. T. Beauregard, First Bull Run, 1861

Alabama soldiers, all I ask of you is to keep
up with the Texans!

—Robert E. Lee, preparing to advance,
the Wilderness, 1864

If you surrender, you shall be treated as
prisoners of war, but if I have to storm your
works, you may expect no quarter.

—Nathan Bedford Forrest

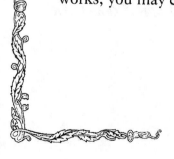

Don't get scared, now that we have got them whipped.

—*James Longstreet to D. H. Hill, Malvern Hill, 1862*

Up, men, and to your posts! Don't forget today you are from Old Virginia.

—*General George Pickett, Gettysburg, 1863*

Colonel Carroll: General, a heavy line of infantry is in our rear. We're between two lines of battle. What'll we do?

General Forrest: Charge both ways!

—*Brice's Cross Roads*

It is well
that war is so
terrible, else men
would learn to love
it too much.

—*Robert E. Lee,
Fredericksburg, 1862*

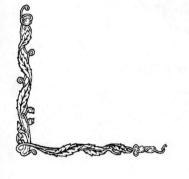

Nathan Bedford Forrest

CHAPTER THREE

Strategy and Tactics

Military scholars point to the War Between the States as the first truly modern war. Their assessment is due in part to the inspired tactical innovations made by Southern commanders to compensate for their lack of troop strength and reliable arms. While the maxims of warfare that follow may sound like common sense, in the thick of battle, they proved to be words of uncommon genius.

An invasion of the enemy's country breaks up all his preconceived plans of invasion.

—*Robert E. Lee*

Once you get them running, you can stay on top of them, and that way a small force can defeat a large one every time.

—*Stonewall Jackson*

War means fighting, and fighting means killing.

—*Nathan Bedford Forrest*

If we can defeat
or drive the armies
of the enemy from the
field, we shall have peace.
All our efforts and energies
should be devoted to
that object.

—*Robert E. Lee to Jefferson Davis,*
July 6, 1864

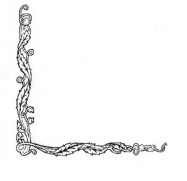

Always mystify, mislead and surprise the enemy; and when you strike and overcome him, never let up in the pursuit. Never fight against heavy odds if you can hurl your own force on only a part of your enemy and crush it. A small army may thus destroy a large one, and repeated victory will make you invincible.

—*Stonewall Jackson*

We have an army far better adapted to attack than to defend. Let us fight at advantage before we are forced to fight at disadvantage.

—*J. E. B. Stuart, 1862*

There has always been a hazard in military movements, but we must decide between the positions of inaction and the risk of action.

—*Robert E. Lee*

It is important that conflict not be provoked until we are ready.

—*Robert E. Lee, 1861*

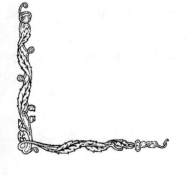

If we cannot be successful in defeating the enemy should he advance, a kind Providence may enable us to inflict a terrible wound and effect a safe retreat in the event of having to fall back.

—*Stonewall Jackson to Joseph E. Johnston, 1862*

The road to glory cannot be followed with much baggage.

—*Richard Stoddert "Dick" Ewell, 1862,
on the necessity of small wagon trains*

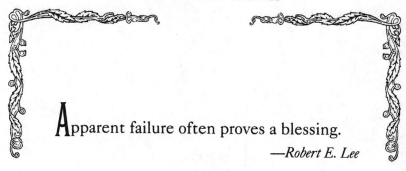

Apparent failure often proves a blessing.

—*Robert E. Lee*

Never stand and take a charge, . . . charge them too.

—*Nathan Bedford Forrest*

Shoot the brave officers, and the cowards will run away and take the men with them.

—*Stonewall Jackson to Dick Ewell*

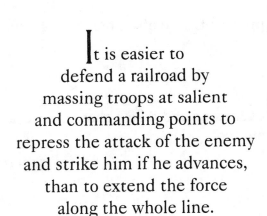

It is easier to
defend a railroad by
massing troops at salient
and commanding points to
repress the attack of the enemy
and strike him if he advances,
than to extend the force
along the whole line.

—*Robert E. Lee*

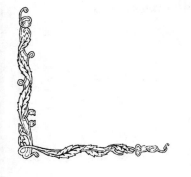
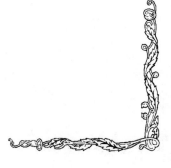

Get there first with the most men.

—Nathan Bedford Forrest

It is sometimes better to wait until you are attacked.

—Robert E. Lee

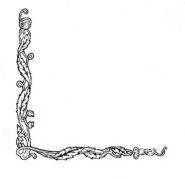
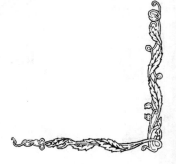

Joseph E. Johnston

CHAPTER FOUR

Leaders of Men

Nothing could do more to improve a soldier's effectiveness than a few heartfelt words of praise and encouragement from his commanding officer. Ranging from martial oratory and edifying counsel to answering the army's critics, these statements encompass all aspects of the unique relationship between commanders and their troops, including what was perhaps the hardest to bear—the transition from war to peace via defeat.

There is only one attitude in which I never should be ashamed of your seeing my men, and that is when they are fighting.

> —*Robert E. Lee, discounting the ragtag appearance of his troops to a British correspondent*

Your little army, derided for its want of arms, derided for its lack of all the essential material of war, has met the grand army of the enemy, routed it at every point, and now it flies, inglorious in retreat before our victorious columns. We have taught them a lesson in their invasion of the sacred soil of Virginia.

> —*President Jefferson Davis, Manassas, Virginia, 1861*

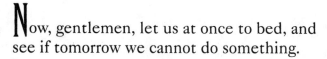

Now, gentlemen, let us at once to bed, and see if tomorrow we cannot do something.

—Stonewall Jackson to his soldiers after a day of profitless marching

Keep steadily in the view of the great principles for which you contend. . . . The safety of your homes and the lives of all you hold dear depend upon your courage and exertions. Let each man resolve to be victorious, and that the right of self-government, liberty and peace shall find him a defender.

—Robert E. Lee's speech to his soldiers, September 9, 1861

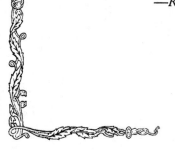

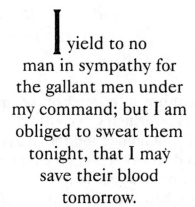

I yield to no
man in sympathy for
the gallant men under
my command; but I am
obliged to sweat them
tonight, that I may
save their blood
tomorrow.

—*Stonewall Jackson, 1862*

I need not tell
the brave survivors of
so many hard-fought battles
who have remained steadfast to
the last that I have consented to this
result from no distrust from them; but
feeling that valor and devotion could
accomplish nothing that could compensate for the loss that attended the continuance of the contest, I determined
to avoid the useless sacrifice of those
whose past services have endeared
them to their countrymen.

—*From Lee's final letter to his men*

I am sorry that the movements of our armies cannot keep pace with the expectations of the editors of the papers. I know they can arrange things satisfactory to themselves on paper. I wish they could do so in the field.

—*Robert E. Lee, 1861*

I will lead you. Follow me.

—*General Joseph E. Johnston*

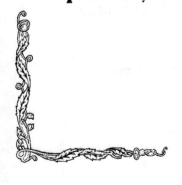

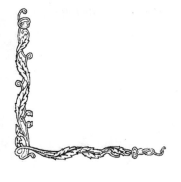

The test of merit in my profession, with the people, is success. It is a hard rule, but I think it right.

—Albert Sidney Johnston, responding to public outcry against him after the loss of Forts Henry and Donelson, 1862

The soldiers know their duties better than the general officers do.

—Robert E. Lee

The army did all it could. I fear I required of it impossibilities.

—Lee absolving the troops of responsibility for failure at Gettysburg, 1863

No matter what may be the ability of the officer, if he loses the confidence of his troops, disaster must sooner or later ensue.

—Lee to Jefferson Davis, 1863

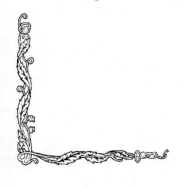

I have never on
the field of battle sent
you where I was unwilling
to go myself, nor would I now
advise you to a course which I felt
myself unwilling to pursue. You have
been good soldiers. You can be good
citizens. Obey the laws, preserve
your honor, and the government
to which you have surrendered
can afford to be and will
be magnanimous.

—*Nathan Bedford Forrest*

I have done the best I could do for you.
Go home now, and if you make as good citizens as you have soldiers, you will do well,
and I shall always be proud of you.
Goodbye, and God bless you all.

—Lee's last words to his troops at Appomattox, 1865

I've got no respect for a young man who
won't join the colors.

—Nathan Bedford Forrest

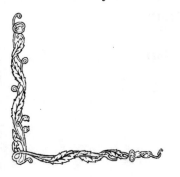

This army stays here until the last wounded man is removed. Before I will leave them to the enemy, I will lose many more men.

—Stonewall Jackson, Winchester, 1862

They have stood it . . . nobly, but if it happens again, I shall join one of their camps and share their wants with them; for I will never allow them to suppose that I feast while they suffer.

—P. G. T. Beauregard, upon learning that some of his regiments were without food, 1861

Close up, men, close up; push on, push on.

—*Stonewall Jackson, his commonly used phrase*

Do your duty in all things. You cannot do more. You should never wish to do less.

—*Robert E. Lee*

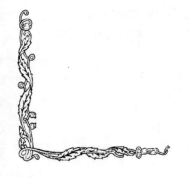

Civil war, such as
you have just passed through,
naturally engenders feelings of
animosity, hatred and revenge. It is
our duty to divest ourselves of all such
feelings, and, so far as it is in our power
to do so, to cultivate feelings toward
those with whom we have so long con-
tested, and heretofore so widely but
honestly differed. Whatever your re-
sponsibilities may be to government,
to society or to individuals,
meet them like men.

—*Nathan Bedford Forrest,
farewell address to his men,
May 9, 1865*

There is a true glory and a true honor: the glory of duty done—the honor of the integrity of principle.

—*Robert E. Lee, Appomattox, 1865*

I have been up to see the Congress, and they don't seem to be able to do anything except eat peanuts and chew tobacco while my army is starving.

—*Robert E. Lee, near the end of the war*

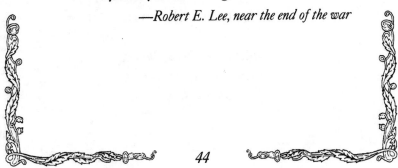

When a man makes a mistake, I call him to my tent, talk to him and use the authority of my position to make him do the right thing next time.

—*Robert E. Lee*

My experience through life has convinced me that, while moderation and temperance in all things is commendable and beneficial, abstinence from spirituous liquors is the best safeguard of morals and health.

—*Robert E. Lee, 1869*

Any man who is in favor of a further prosecution of this war is a fit subject for a lunatic asylum, and ought to be sent there immediately.

—*Nathan Bedford Forrest*

Never take counsel of your fears.

—*Stonewall Jackson*

Young gentleman, we have no printed rules. We have but one rule here, and it is that every student must be a gentleman.

—*Robert E. Lee, as president of Washington College*

We gain successes but after every fight there comes in to me an ominous paper marked "casualties," "killed" and "wounded." Sad words which carry anguish to so many hearts. And we have scarcely time to bury the dead as we push on in the same deadly strife.

—*Wade Hampton, letter to his sister, 1864*

Whatever happens, know this, that no men ever fought better than those who have stood by me.

—*Robert E. Lee, Clover Hill, 1865*

J. E. B. Stuart

CHAPTER FIVE

Among Their Peers

The effectiveness of the Confederate high command was impaired by numerous personality conflicts. However, at a time when a generation of commanders considered Napoleon to be the military ideal, the situation perhaps could have been worse. Lee's comportment, in fact, proved him to be anything but an egomaniac. Critics contend that he was polite and accommodating to stubborn, shortsighted subordinates, while lesser talents like Bragg and Beauregard could be unbelievably petty and recalcitrant. But if there was frustration, there was also glory, as exemplified by the rare coordination of purpose between Lee and Jackson, and Forrest's stunning successes despite his gains being underexploited by inept superiors.

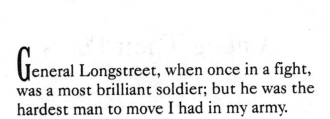

General Longstreet, when once in a fight, was a most brilliant soldier; but he was the hardest man to move I had in my army.

—*Robert E. Lee*

I know not how to replace him.

—*Robert E. Lee at Stonewall Jackson's funeral*

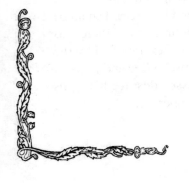

If I had had Stonewall Jackson with me, so far as man can see, I should have won the battle of Gettysburg.

—*Robert E. Lee*

Such an executive officer the sun never shone on. I have but to show him my design, and I know that it can be done, it will be done. . . . Straight as the needle to the pole he advanced to the execution of my purpose.

—*Robert E. Lee on Stonewall Jackson*

I will be in my coffin before I will fight again under your command.

—*Nathan Bedford Forrest to Joe Wheeler*

Colonel Walker, did it ever occur to you that General Jackson is crazy?

—*Dick Ewell*

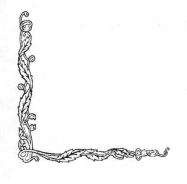
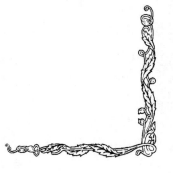

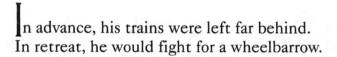

In advance, his trains were left far behind.
In retreat, he would fight for a wheelbarrow.

—*Dick Taylor on Stonewall Jackson*

The shot that struck me down is the very best that has been fired for the Southern cause yet. For I possess in no degree the confidence of our government, and now they have in my place someone who does . . . and who can accomplish what I never could have done—the concentration of our armies for the defense of the capital of the Confederacy.

—*A wounded Joseph E. Johnston upon Robert E. Lee's assumption of command of the Army of Northern Virginia*

If you ever again try to interfere with me or cross my path, it will be at the peril of your life.

—*Nathan Bedford Forrest to Braxton Bragg*

A man I have never seen, sir. His name is Forrest.

—*Robert E. Lee's response when asked who was the greatest soldier under his command, Appomattox, 1865*

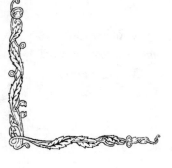

I do not mean to say that he is not competent, but from what I have seen of him I do not know that he is.

—Robert E. Lee of his artillery chief,
General W. N. Pendleton

The general is a little nervous this morning; he wishes me to attack; I do not wish to do so without Pickett. I never like to go into battle with one boot off.

—James Longstreet on Robert E. Lee, Gettysburg, 1863

A. P. Hill

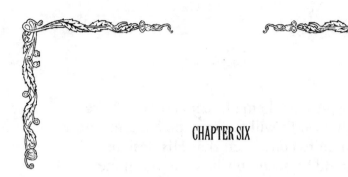

CHAPTER SIX

Faith and Doubt

When Confederate commanders invoked the name of God, it was the Old Testament Jehovah they had in mind. Lee and Jackson, two men of unshakable faith, always attributed their success to Him. But they shouldered responsibility for the failures themselves. They alternated between the certainty of their simple Christian convictions and bleak moments of self-doubt.

At present, I am not concerned with results. God's will ought to be our aim, and I am quite contented that His designs should be accomplished and not mine.

—*Robert E. Lee, 1861*

Our God was my shield. His protecting care is an additional cause for gratitude.

—*Stonewall Jackson, Winchester, 1862*

I am truly grateful to the Giver of Victory for having blessed us in our terrible struggle. I pray He may continue.

—*Robert E. Lee to Stonewall Jackson, 1862*

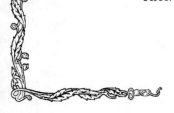

So far as I can see, my course was a wise one; the best that I could do under the circumstances, though very distasteful to my feelings; and I hope and pray to Our Heavenly Father that I may never again be circumstanced as on that day.

—Stonewall Jackson after fighting a battle on Sunday, Winchester, 1862

How easily I could be rid of this, and be at rest. I have only to ride along the line and all will be over.

—Robert E. Lee on the morning of Appomattox, 1865

Sacrifices! Have I not made them? What is my life here but a daily sacrifice?

—Stonewall Jackson, in a resignation letter that was never acted upon, 1862

Our enemies are pressing us everywhere. . . . I pray that the great God may aid us, and am endeavoring by every means in my power to bring out the troops and hasten them to their destination.

—Robert E. Lee, 1862

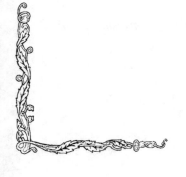

I tremble for my
country when I hear of
confidence expressed in me.
I know too well my weakness,
that our only hope is
in God.

—*Robert E. Lee to his wife, 1862*

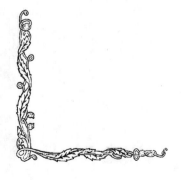
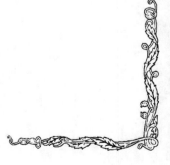

If you desire to be more heavenly minded, think more of the things of heaven, and less of the things of earth.

—*Stonewall Jackson*

I can only say that I am nothing but a poor sinner, trusting in Christ alone for salvation.

—*Robert E. Lee*

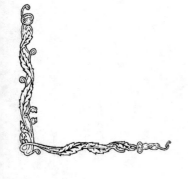
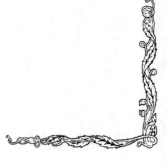

I am too old to command this army. We should never have permitted [the enemy] to get away.

—*Robert E. Lee*

After it is all over, as stupid a fellow as I am can see the mistakes that were made. I notice, however, that my mistakes are never told me until it is too late.

—*Robert E. Lee to his officers after Gettysburg, 1863*

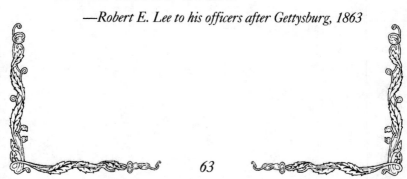

No, you greatly overestimate my capacity for usefulness. A better man will soon be sent to take my place.

—Stonewall Jackson, 1861

Colonel, when I lose my temper, don't let it make you angry.

—Robert E. Lee to his military secretary

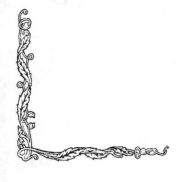

Conscious of
my imperfections and
the little claim I have to be
classed among Christians, I know
the temptations and trials I shall have
to pass through. May God enable me
to perform my duty and not suffer
me to be tempted beyond
my strength.

—*Robert E. Lee, 1861*

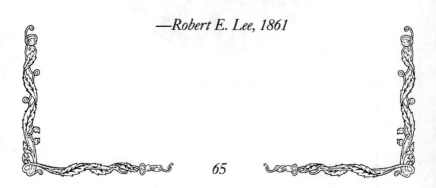

Stonewall Jackson

CHAPTER SEVEN

Aftermath

Troubled by the ominous outlook of the region's imminent political fortunes, leading figures of the Southern cause adopted a message of reunion and reconciliation in the years following the war.

✴ ✴ ✴

I believe it to
be the duty of everyone
to unite in the restoration of the
country and the reestablishment
of peace and harmony.

—*Robert E. Lee*

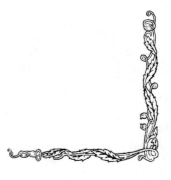

I believe I may say,
looking into my own heart,
and speaking as in the presence
of God, that I have never known
one moment of bitterness
or resentment.

—*Robert E. Lee, commenting on his feelings*
toward the North after the war

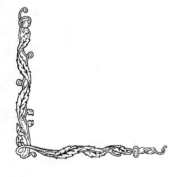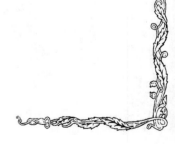

We must look to the rising generation for the restoration of the country.

—Robert E. Lee to Governor John Letcher, August 1865

I have fought against the people of the North because I believed they were seeking to wrest from the South its dearest right. But I have never cherished toward them bitter or vindictive feelings, and I have never seen the day when I did not pray for them.

—Robert E. Lee

The past is dead:
let it bury its dead, its hopes
and its aspirations; before you
lies the future—a future full
of golden promise.

—*Jefferson Davis*

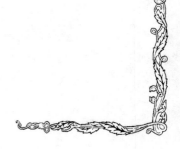

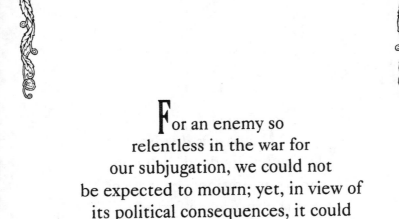

For an enemy so relentless in the war for our subjugation, we could not be expected to mourn; yet, in view of its political consequences, it could not be regarded otherwise than as a great misfortune for the South.

—*Jefferson Davis on the assassination of Lincoln*

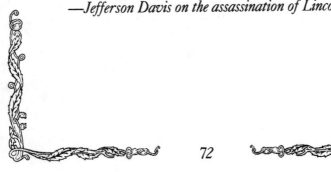

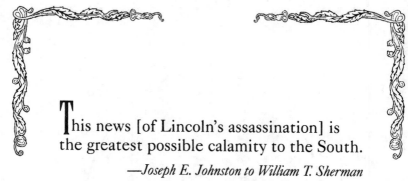

This news [of Lincoln's assassination] is the greatest possible calamity to the South.

—*Joseph E. Johnston to William T. Sherman*

This is not the fate to which I invited you when the future was rose-colored for us both; but I know you will bear it even better than myself, and that, of us two, I alone will ever look back reproachfully on my career.

—*Jefferson Davis to his wife from his prison cell at Fortress Monroe, 1865*

P. G. T. Beauregard

Last Tattoo

Their final words are a ready source of endless fascination. Some had the luxury of longer reflection, along with the obligation to eulogize those who died before them. Many met their end sooner on the battlefield.

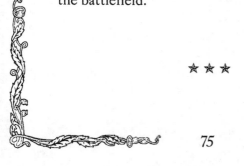

★ ★ ★

Death, in its silent,
sure march is fast gathering those
whom I have longest loved, so that
when he shall knock at my door, I
will more willingly follow.

—*Robert E. Lee, 1869*

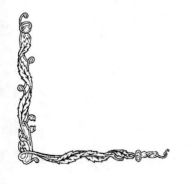

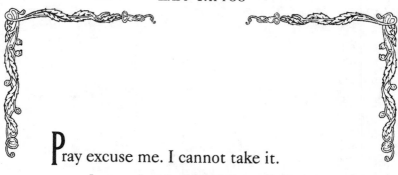

Pray excuse me. I cannot take it.

—Last words of President Jefferson Davis, refusing to take medicine on his deathbed, December 6, 1889

Go back, go back and do your duty, as I have done mine, and our country will be safe. Go back, go back . . . I had rather die than be whipped.

—A mortally wounded J. E. B. Stuart exhorting his troops to fight on without him

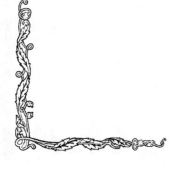

He is now at rest,
and we who are left are the
ones to suffer.

—*Robert E. Lee on the death of A. P. Hill,*
Petersburg, 1865

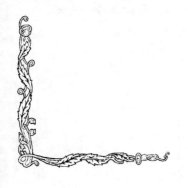
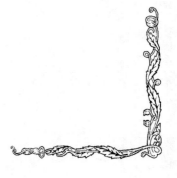

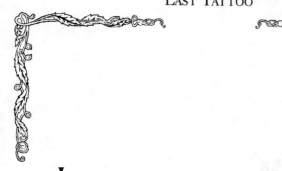
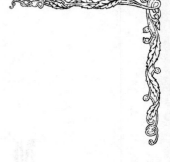

Let us pass over the river and rest under the shade of the trees.

—Stonewall Jackson's last words at the Battle of Chancellorsville, 1863

Strike the tent!

—Robert E. Lee's final words, October 12, 1870

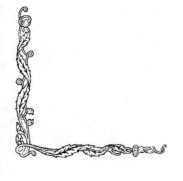

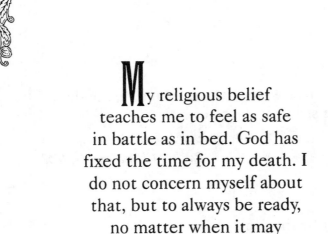

My religious belief
teaches me to feel as safe
in battle as in bed. God has
fixed the time for my death. I
do not concern myself about
that, but to always be ready,
no matter when it may
overtake me.

—*Stonewall Jackson*

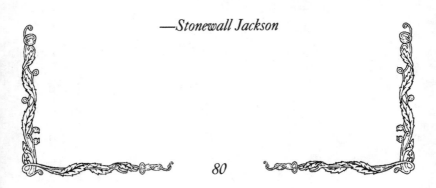

W ell, if we are to die,
let us die like men.

*—Last reported words of
Pat Cleburne, Franklin, 1864*

Without doing
injustice to the living,
it may safely be asserted
that our loss is irreparable; and
that among the shining hosts of the
great and good who now cluster around
the banner of the country, there exists
no purer spirit, no more heroic soul,
than that of the illustrious man
whose death I join you
in lamenting.

—Jefferson Davis grieving the death of
General Albert Sidney Johnston, 1862

I shall come out of this fight a live major general or a dead brigadier.

  —Brigadier General Albert Perrin, killed in action at the
              Battle of Spotsylvania

Governor Harris: General, are you wounded?

General Johnston: Yes, and I fear seriously.

  —Last words of Albert Sidney Johnston, who bled to
    death at Shiloh, 1862, after being struck by a
      stray minié ball. A simple tourniquet
        could have saved his life.

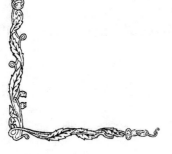

The truth is this:
The march of Providence
is so slow and our desires so
impatient; the work of progress
is so immense and our means of
aiding it so feeble; the life of humanity
is so long, that of the individual so
brief, that we often see only the
ebb of the advancing wave and
are thus discouraged. It is
history that teaches us
to hope.

—*Robert E. Lee, near the end of his life*

MAY I QUOTE YOU, GENERAL LEE?

Volume Two

To my wife, Amanda Bedwell

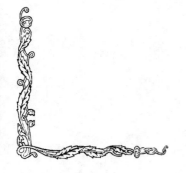
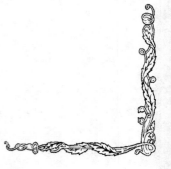

Table of Contents

Robert E. Lee was one
of the small company of great men
in whom there was no inconsistency to
be explained, no enigma to be solved. What
he seemed, he was—a wholly human gentleman,
the essential elements of whose positive
character were two and only two,
simplicity and spirituality.

*—Douglas Southall Freeman,
Robert E. Lee's biographer*

Introduction

The statements on these pages are among the most moving and insightful ever to express what Oliver Wendell Holmes Jr. called "the incommunicable experience of war." The South's great generals knew they were commissioned not only to win battles—though they did strive heroically and often triumphantly for victory. They were equally entrusted with a sacred responsibility to uphold duty and honor. Following the principled example set by General Robert E. Lee, the Southern command was characterized by gallantry and chivalry in the face of overwhelming odds. The Confederate generals represent a tradition that is now as far removed from contemporary experience as the way of life they fought to preserve. Their words are an immortal testament to their dignity.

Randall Bedwell
Nashville, Tennessee
October 1998

General Robert E. Lee

CHAPTER ONE

The Grim Prelude

In the days and weeks before discord boiled over into war, the generals and executives of the Confederacy refrained from inflammatory rhetoric. They could not indulge in the heady, reckless posturing adopted by so many private citizens during that period. The commanders knew what lay ahead. They knew their words would have consequence.

Instead of boasts and swagger, the South's sage leaders counseled temperance and reason. They viewed war as the sum of all evils. They warned of the North's determination and underlying strength, and the folly of firing on Fort Sumter.

Yet, their self-restraint never reflected any attempt to shirk their duty. In the end, service to their homeland decided their course.

***

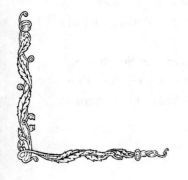

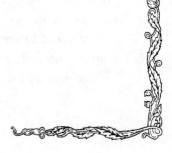

Secession is nothing but revolution. Still, a union that can only be maintained by swords and bayonets, and in which strife and civil war are to take the place of brotherly love and kindness, has no charm for me. If the Union is dissolved, the government disrupted, I shall return to my native state and share the miseries of my people. Save in her defense, I will draw my sword no more.

—Robert E. Lee, in a letter to his son, 1861

All we ask is to be let alone.

—*Jefferson Davis, president,*
Confederate States of America

It is painful enough to discover with what unconcern they speak of war and threaten it. I have seen enough of it to make me look upon it as the sum of all evils.

—*Stonewall Jackson, 1861*

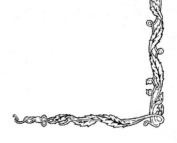

[If the] Northern states…desire to inflict injury upon us…a terrible responsibility will rest upon it, and the suffering of millions will bear testimony to the folly and wickedness of our aggressors.

—Jefferson Davis, inaugural address as provisional president of the Southern Confederacy, February 18, 1861

I am in favor of making a thorough trial for peace, and if we fail in this and our state is invaded, to defend it with terrific resistance.

—Stonewall Jackson to his nephew, January 1861

The North is determined to preserve this Union. They are not a fiery, impulsive people as you are, for they live in colder climates, but when they begin to move in a given direction, they move with the steady momentum and perseverance of an avalanche.

—Texas Governor Sam Houston, 1861

Unless you sprinkle blood in the face of the Southern people, they will be back in the old Union in less than ten days.

—An advisor to Jefferson Davis

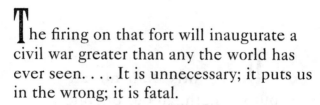

The firing on that fort will inaugurate a civil war greater than any the world has ever seen. . . . It is unnecessary; it puts us in the wrong; it is fatal.

> —*Confederate Secretary of State Robert Toombs*

I cannot raise my hand against my birthplace, my home, my children.

> —*Robert E. Lee, in his letter of resignation from the U.S. Army*

I think it better to do right, even if we suffer in so doing, than to incur the reproach of our consciences and posterity.

> —*Robert E. Lee*

Our country demands all our strength, all our energies. To resist the powerful combination now forming against us will require every man at his place. If victorious, we have everything to hope for in the future. If defeated, nothing will be left for us to live for. My whole trust is in God, and I am ready for whatever He may ordain.

—*Robert E. Lee, in a letter to one of his sons*

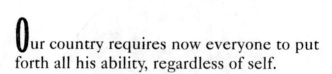

Our country requires now everyone to put forth all his ability, regardless of self.

—Robert E. Lee, to one of his sons in 1861

All I am and all I have is at the service of my country.

—Stonewall Jackson, 1861

I prefer annihilation to submission. They may destroy but I trust never conquer us.

—Robert E. Lee to a relative, 1861

James Longstreet

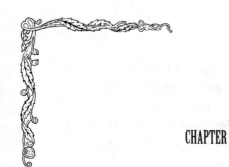

CHAPTER TWO

Under Fire

In the stress of battle, many prewar reputations were the first casualties. Braggadocio proved useless against the Union cannonade for many classroom and armchair generals. Nonetheless, the slow-to-anger Southern command typified by the fighting style of Robert E. Lee displayed an unshakable courage in combat that is admired and even emulated to this day.

When the battle call sounded, the generals answered. They led their charges to where the fire

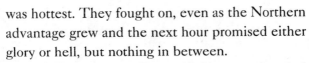

was hottest. They fought on, even as the Northern advantage grew and the next hour promised either glory or hell, but nothing in between.

These wartime leaders and the men they led dedicated themselves to preserving the South even if it cost them their lives.

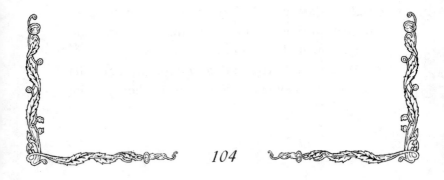

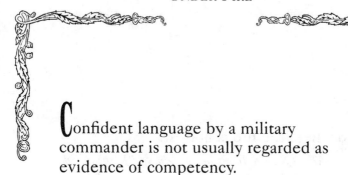

Confident language by a military commander is not usually regarded as evidence of competency.

—*Albert Sidney Johnston*

We will breakfast together here and dine together in hell.

—*Richard Stoddert Ewell at First Manassas*

The battle is there. I am going.

—*Albert Sidney Johnston to P. G. T. Beauregard at First Manassas, July 1861*

Go where the fire is hottest.
—*Albert Sidney Johnston to Edmund Kirby Smith*
at First Manassas, July 1861

Charge, men, and yell like furies!
—*Stonewall Jackson to his troops at*
First Manassas, July 1861

This is a hard fight and we had better all die than lose it.
—*General James Longstreet, Antietam, 1862*

As each brigade
emerged from the woods,
from 50 to 100 guns opened
upon it, tearing great gaps in its
ranks; but the heroes pressed on
and were shot down by reserves
at the guns. It was not war; it
was murder.

—D. H. Hill on the battle of Malvern Hill, 1862

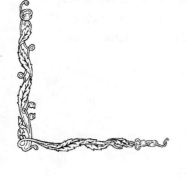

These men are going to stay here, General, 'till the sun goes down or victory is won.

—John Gordon to Lee at Sharpsburg, 1862

General, you have my hat and plume. I have your blue coat. I have the honor to propose a cartel for a fair exchange of the prisoners.

—General J. E. B. Stuart to John Pope after Stuart had lost his hat on a raid behind Pope's lines but had stolen the Union general's new coat in a supply dump. Second Manassas 1862

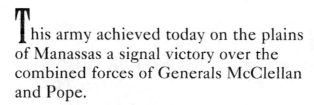

This army achieved today on the plains of Manassas a signal victory over the combined forces of Generals McClellan and Pope.

—General Lee to President Davis on the victory at Second Manassas, 1862

I think you hurt them as much as they hurt you.

—Longstreet to Lee on the Peninsula campaign and Seven Days' Battles in 1862

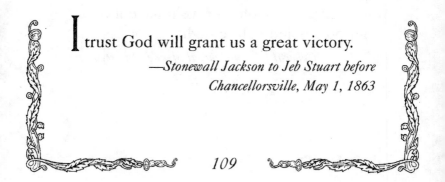

I trust God will grant us a great victory.

—Stonewall Jackson to Jeb Stuart before Chancellorsville, May 1, 1863

109

If he is there tomorrow, I will attack him.

> —*General Lee referring to*
> *General Meade at Gettysburg*

In an hour, you'll be in hell or glory.

> —*General Cadmus Marcellus Wilcox to*
> *General George Pickett at Gettysburg, 1863*

General Meade might as well have saved himself the trouble, for we'll have it in our possession before night.

> —*General Lee on General Meade at Gettysburg*

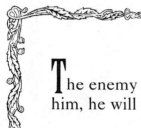

The enemy is here and if we do not whip him, he will whip us.

—*General Lee to General John Bell Hood at Gettysburg, 1863*

General, if you are to advance at all, you must come at once or we will not be able to support you as we ought. . . . For God's sake, come quick.

—*E. P. Alexander to General Longstreet at Gettysburg just before Pickett's Charge*

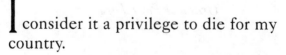

I consider it a privilege to die for my country.

—*Brigadier General Paul John Semmes, after being wounded at Gettysburg, July 1863*

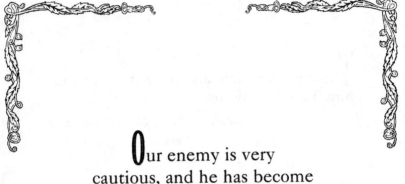

Our enemy is very cautious, and he has become so proficient in entrenching that he seems to march with a system already prepared. He threatens dreadful things every day, but, thank God, has not expunged us yet.

—*General Lee on General Grant at Petersburg*

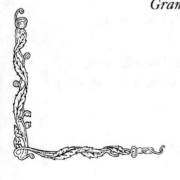

Attention, Texas Brigade! The eyes of General Lee are upon you. Forward, march!

—General Maxcy Gregg at the Wilderness in 1864

Face the fire and go in where it is hottest!

—General A. P. Hill, May 1864

Nathan Bedford Forrest

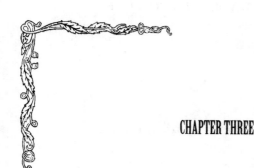

CHAPTER THREE

Exemplary Conduct

In war as in peace, Robert E. Lee conducted himself in a manner that inspired devotion and emulation from his soldiers and fellow officers. His men considered him an agent of God, placed in their midst not only to lead them through battle but also toward a higher calling.

Although unassuming in manner and dress, Lee won the respect of both the soldiers under his command and those who fought against him. He was a man of patience, moderation and fortitude.

Throughout the struggle between the states, Lee counseled the South to maintain honor, duty and hope, even in its darkest hour.

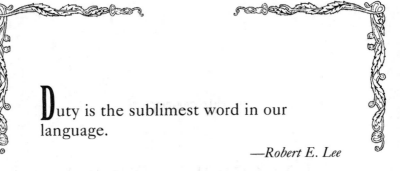

Duty is the sublimest word in our language.

—*Robert E. Lee*

The idea of his life was to do his duty, at whatever the cost, and to try to help others do theirs.

—*Robert E. Lee Jr., on his father*

Do your duty. That is all the pleasure, all the comfort, all the glory we can enjoy in this world.

—*Robert E. Lee*

[Lee] came back, carrying the heavy weight of defeat, and unappreciated by the people, for they could not know that, if his plans had been carried out, the result would have been victory. Yet, through all this, he stood in silence, without defending himself for he was unwilling to offend any one who was wearing a sword and striking a blow for the Confederacy.

—Jefferson Davis on Lee in 1861 after Lee's campaign into the Shenandoah Valley

It will give me great pleasure to do everything I can to relieve him and serve the country, but I do not see either advantage or pleasure in my duties.

—General Lee writing in a letter to his wife about his replacing General Joseph Johnston, who had been wounded at Seven Pines, 1862

What is life without honor? Degradation is worse than death.

—Stonewall Jackson to an officer who had requested a leave to visit a sick relative.

I shall endeavor to do my duty and fight to the last.

—General Lee, in a letter to his wife, 1865

Duty is ours; consequences are God's.

—Stonewall Jackson

What do you care about rank? I would serve under a corporal if necessary!

—General Lee's reproach to a
subordinate eager for promotion

But what care can a man give to himself in time of war? It is from no desire of exposure or hazard that I live in a tent, but from necessity. I must be where I can speedily attend to the duties of my position, and be near or accessible to the officers with whom I have to act.

—General Lee, in a letter to his wife,
September 18, 1864

Eight million people turned their eyes to Lexington seeking instructions and paternal advice in the severe trials they have to undergo. They read in the example of General Lee . . . the lessons of patience, moderation, fortitude, and earnest devotion to the requirements of duty, which are the only safe guides to them in their troubles. His history, his present labors, and his calm confidence in the future kindle the flames of hope in the hearts of millions, that else all would be darkness.

*—John M. Morgan commenting on
Robert E. Lee's unique position in
the national consciousness after the war*

I am as willing to serve now as in the beginning in any capacity and at any post where I can do good. The lower the position, the more suitable to my ability and the more agreeable to my feelings.

—*General Lee to Jefferson Davis,*
after the Gettysburg defeat, 1863

My chief concern is to try to be an humble, sincere Christian.

—*Robert E. Lee*

Intellectually, he was cast in a giant mold. Naturally he was possessed of strong passions. He loved excitement, particularly the excitement of war. He loved grandeur. But all these appetites and powers were brought under the control of his judgment and made subservient to his Christian faith. This made him habitually unselfish and ever willing to sacrifice on the altar of duty and in the service of his fellows. . . . He is an epistle, written of God and designed by God to teach the people of this country that earthly success is not the criterion of merit, not the measure of true greatness.

—*General John Gordon on Robert E. Lee*

I can only say that I am nothing but a poor sinner, trusting in Christ alone for salvation, and need all of the prayers they can offer for me.

—*General Lee's response when told that the army chaplains were daily praying for him.*

I hope we will yet be able to damage our adversaries when they meet us. That it should be so, we must implore the forgiveness of God for our sins, and the continuance of his blessings.

—*Robert E. Lee*

The advantages of the enemy will have little value if we permit them to impair our resolution. Let us then oppose them with the firm assurance that He who gave freedom to our fathers will bless the efforts of their children.

—*Robert E. Lee, 1865*

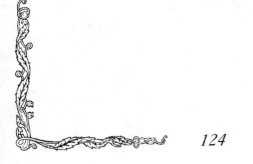
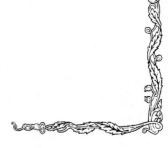

What a glorious world God Almighty has given us. How thankless and ungrateful we are, and how we labor to mar His gifts.

—Robert E. Lee

Mark the perfect man, and behold the upright; for the end of that man is peace."

—Psalm 37. William Nelson Pendleton (former Confederate chaplain) composed Lee's eulogy around this Bible passage

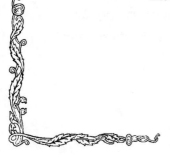

Through the broad extent of country over which you have marched by your respect for the rights and property of citizens, you have shown that you were soldiers not only to defend but able and willing both to defend and protect.

—*Stonewall Jackson to his troops, 1861*

I have never witnessed on any previous occasion such entire disregard of the usage of civilized warfare and the dictates of humanity.

—*General Lee, in a report concerning Union destruction of civilian property in Virginia, 1863*

All I ever wanted was a Virginia farm, no end of cream and fresh butter and fried chicken—not one fried chicken, or two, but unlimited fried chicken.

—General Lee bantering with Mary Boykin Chesnut and friends just after First Manassas

General Jubal Early to General Lee: I wish they were all dead.

Lee to Early: Why, I do not wish that they were all dead. I merely wish that they would return to their homes and leave us in peace.

Early, after Lee departed: I would not say so in front of General Lee, but I wish that they were not only dead but in hell.

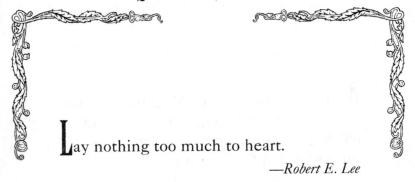

Lay nothing too much to heart.

—*Robert E. Lee*

Human virtue should be equal to human calamity.

—*Robert E. Lee*

It is only the ignorant who suppose themselves omniscient.

—*Robert E. Lee*

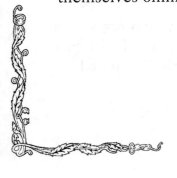

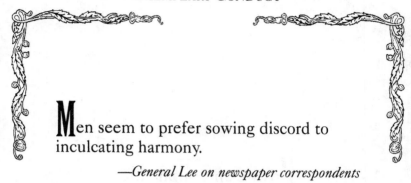

Men seem to prefer sowing discord to inculcating harmony.

—General Lee on newspaper correspondents

We have only one rule here—to act like a gentleman at all times.

—General Lee's only rule as president
of Washington College

A true man of honor feels humble himself when he cannot help humbling others.

—Robert E. Lee

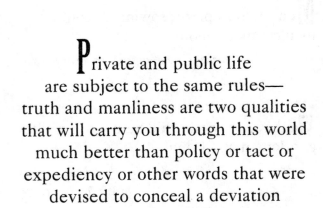

Private and public life
are subject to the same rules—
truth and manliness are two qualities
that will carry you through this world
much better than policy or tact or
expediency or other words that were
devised to conceal a deviation
from a straight line.

—*Robert E. Lee*

As a general principle, you should not force young men to do their duty, but let them do it voluntarily and thereby develop their characters.

—Robert E. Lee

The trite saying that honesty is the best policy has met with the just criticism that honesty is not policy. The real honest man is honest from conviction of what is right, not from policy.

—Robert E. Lee

Say what you mean to
do . . . and take it for granted
that you mean to do right. Never
do a wrong thing to make a friend or
keep one . . . you will wrong him and
wrong yourself by equivocation
of any kind.

—*Robert E. Lee*

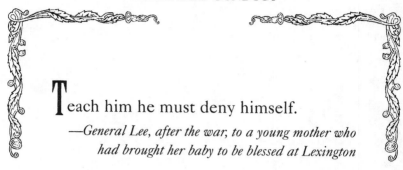

Teach him he must deny himself.

—*General Lee, after the war, to a young mother who had brought her baby to be blessed at Lexington*

Practice self-denial and self-control, as well as the strictest economy in all financial matters.

—*Robert E. Lee*

He exhibited no external signs of his rank, his dress being a plain suit of gray. His office was simply furnished with plain desks and chairs.

—*A. L. Long on Lee*

Read history, works
of truth, not novels and romances.
Get correct views of life, and learn to
see the world in its true light. It will
enable you to live pleasantly, to do
good and, when summoned away,
to leave without regret.

—*Robert E. Lee*

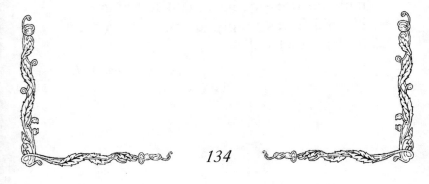

The education of a man or woman is never completed until they die.

—*Robert E. Lee*

He exhibited no external signs of his rank, his dress being a plain suit of gray. His office was simply furnished with plain desks and chairs.

—*A. L. Long on Lee in 1861*

You don't care for military glory or fame, but we are proud of your name and the record of this army. We want to leave it to our children. . . . A little blood, more or less, now makes no difference.

—*E. P. Alexander to Lee at Appomattox*

Joseph E. Johnston

CHAPTER FOUR

The Craft of War

Outnumbered and undersupplied, the South's generals employed innovative battle strategies that were often so brilliant they have been studied and utilized by military strategists for more than a century. Regardless of the circumstances, these Southern commanders resolutely directed their troops in a manner that would become legend.

Ultimately, however, the South's greatest generals are remembered most not for their military strategies but rather for their unwavering devotion to the basic tenets of duty.

His name might be Audacity. He will take more desperate chances and take them quicker than any other general in the country, North or South.

—*General Ives on Lee*

McClellan will make this a battle of posts. He will take position from position, under cover of his heavy artillery, and we cannot get at him without storming his works, which with our new troops is extremely hazardous.

—*General Lee to Davis prior to the Seven Days' Battles, June 1862*

I am aware that the movement is attended with much risk, yet I do not consider success impossible, and shall endeavor to guard it from loss. . . . What occasions me most is the fear of getting out of ammunition.

—General Lee to President Davis on
the Maryland invasion, 1862

We can only act upon probabilities and endeavor to avoid greater evils.

—General Lee, in a letter to Stonewall Jackson

We must expect reverses, even defeats. They are sent to teach us wisdom and prudence, to call forth greater energies, and to prevent our falling into greater disasters.

—*Robert E. Lee*

So great is my confidence in General Lee that I am willing to follow him blindfolded.

—*Stonewall Jackson*

My interference in battle
would do more harm than good.
I have then to rely on my brigade and
division commanders. I think and work
with all my power to bring the troops
to the right place at the right time;
then I have done my duty. As soon as I
order them forward into battle. I leave
my duty in the hands of God.

—*Robert E. Lee*

If officers desire to have control over their commands, they must remain habitually with them, industriously attend to their instruction and comfort, and in battle lead them well.

—*Stonewall Jackson to his commanders, 1861*

Keep your command together and in good spirits, General; don't let it think of surrender. I will get you out of this.

—*General Lee to Fitz Lee on the retreat from Petersburg*

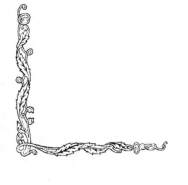

We may be annihilated, but we cannot be conquered.

—*General Lee, in a letter to his brother, 1862*

It is always well to expect the enemy to do what he should do.

—*saying attributed to Lee*

To move swiftly, strike vigorously, and secure all the fruits of victory is the secret of a successful war.

—*Stonewall Jackson, 1863*

I had rather lose one man in marching than five in fighting.

—*Stonewall Jackson*

Don't scatter your forces. There is one rule in our profession that should never be forgotten—it is to throw the masses of your troops on the fractions of the enemy.

—*William Joseph Hardee to Braxton Bragg, October 7, 1862*

Arms is a profession that, if its principles are adhered to for success, requires an officer do what he fears may be wrong and yet, according to military experience, must be done, if success is to be attained.

—*Stonewall Jackson, in a letter to his wife, 1862*

James Ewell Brown "Jeb" Stuart

CHAPTER FIVE

Lost Opportunities

Despite the storied exploits of Confederate troops that are retold and passed from generation to generation, there were also moments of hesitation and indecision that plagued the Southern command. In hindsight, the outcome of Gettysburg, and perhaps even the war, might have been different if other actions had been taken.

Unfortunately for them, generals are not granted the luxury of making their decisions in hindsight. Once written, history marches on, oblivious to all else that might have been.

Lee never tried to avoid blame; in fact, he insisted on shouldering more than he deserved. Most military historians have not judged him harshly; indeed, many consider him the greatest commander on either side of the war.

Our people have thought too much of themselves and their ease, and instead of turning out to a man, have been content to nurse themselves and their dimes and leave the protection of themselves and their families to others. . . . This is not the way to accomplish our independence.

—*General Lee from South Carolina in 1861*

I know Mr. Davis thinks that he can do a great many things that other men would hesitate to attempt. For instance, he tried to do what God had failed to do. He tried to make a soldier out of Braxton Bragg, and you know the result. It couldn't be done.

—*General Joseph Johnston*

When this war began I was opposed to it, bitterly opposed to it, and I told these people that unless every man should do his whole duty, they would repent it. And now they will repent.

—*General Lee speaking to his son Custis at Richmond in 1865*

The Confederate chief at Gettysburg looked something like Napoleon at Waterloo.

—*James Longstreet on Lee*

If I had taken General Longstreet's advice on the eve of the second day of the battle of Gettysburg . . . [then] the Confederates would today be a free people.

—*Robert E. Lee*

Come General Pickett . . . this has been my fight and upon my shoulders rests the blame. The men and officers of your command have written the name of Virginia as high today as it has ever been written before.

—*General Lee at Gettysburg*

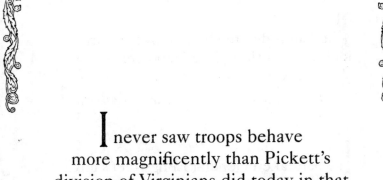

I never saw troops behave more magnificently than Pickett's division of Virginians did today in that grand charge upon the enemy. And if they had been supported as they were to have been, the day would have been ours.

—*General Lee at Gettysburg*

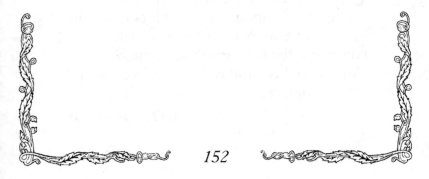

Over the splendid scene of human courage and human sacrifice at Gettysburg there arises in the South an apparition, like Banquo's ghost at Macbeth's banquet, which says the battle was lost to the Confederates because someone blundered.

—*Fitzhugh Lee*

If victorious, we have everything to live for. If defeated, there will be nothing left to live for.

—*General Lee, commenting on the outcome of the Wilderness campaign, 1863*

153

Stonewall Jackson

CHAPTER SIX

A Dignified Defeat

After four long years on the march and in battle, Lee faced the end in the spring of 1865. It was a conclusion the general had fought against with unsurpassed courage and fortitude despite overwhelming enemy numbers and superior resources. He declared he would rather "die a thousand deaths" than surrender.

With the eyes of the world watching, the Southern commanders and troops met the end with bitter tears, heads bowed, and heavy hearts.

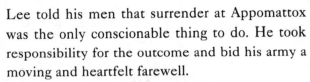

Lee told his men that surrender at Appomattox was the only conscionable thing to do. He took responsibility for the outcome and bid his army a moving and heartfelt farewell.

With that, Lee mounted his horse and rode away down a road lined with tearful Confederate soldiers.

★ ★ ★

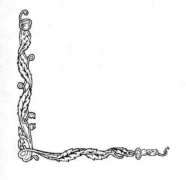

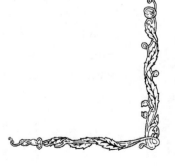

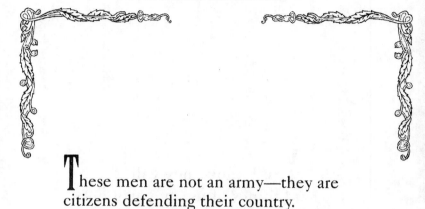

These men are not an army—they are citizens defending their country.

—Robert E. Lee

There is a true glory and a true honor; the glory of duty done—and the honor of the integrity of the principle.

—Robert E. Lee

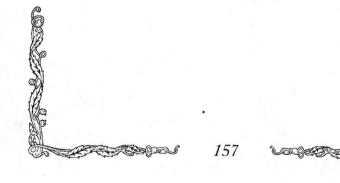

Yes, I know they will
say hard things of us; they will not
understand how we were overwhelmed
by numbers. But that is not the
question, Colonel; the question is,
"Is it right to surrender this army?" If
it is right, then I will take all
the responsibility.

—*General Lee at Appomattox*

There is nothing left me but to go and see General Grant, and I would rather die a thousand deaths.

—General Lee on the morning of April 9, 1865

As you are now more reasonable, I will say that General Lee has gone to meet General Grant, and it is for them to determine the future of our armies.

—James Longstreet to General George A. Custer at Appomattox in response to the demand that Longstreet surrender the Army of Northern Virginia, April 9, 1865

After four years of arduous service marked by unsurpassed courage and fortitude, the Army of Northern Virginia has been compelled to yield to overwhelming numbers and resources. With an unceasing admiration of your constancy and devotion to your country, and a grateful remembrance of your kind and generous consideration for myself, I bid you an affectionate farewell.

—*General Lee's farewell address to his army,*
April 10, 1865

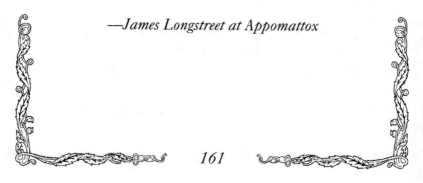

The road was packed by standing troops as he approached, the men with hats off, heads and hearts bowed down. As he passed, they raised their heads and looked upon him with swimming eyes. Those who could find voice said goodbye; those who could not speak, and were near, passed their hands gently over the sides of Traveller.

—James Longstreet at Appomattox

Lee: What are you doing with all that gray in your beard?

Meade: You have to answer for most of it.

—*April 10, 1865*

His continued self-denial can only be explained upon the hypothesis that he desired his men to know that he shared their privations to the very end.

—*Walter Taylor on General Lee en route to Richmond after Appomattox*

It is utterly impossible, Mister Brady. How can I sit for a photograph with the eyes of the world upon me as they are today?

—*General Lee to Matthew Brady at Richmond in 1865*

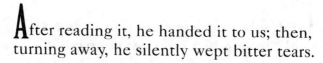

After reading it, he handed it to us; then, turning away, he silently wept bitter tears.

> —*Robert E. Lee III describing Jefferson Davis's reaction to the news of Lee's surrender to Grant*

If I live, you can come to me when the struggle has ended, but I do not expect to survive the destruction of constitutional liberty.

> —*Jefferson Davis's parting words to his wife before the fall of Richmond*

We had, I was satisfied, sacred principles to maintain and rights to defend, for which we were in duty bound to do our best, even if we perished in the endeavor.

> —*General Lee at the close of the war*

I did only what my duty demanded. I could have taken no other course without dishonor. And if all were to be done over again, I should act in precisely the same manner.

—*Robert E. Lee*

It is fair to assume that the strongest laws are those established by the sword. The ideas that divided political parties before the war—upon the rights of states—were thoroughly discussed by our wisest statesmen, and eventually appealed to the arbitrament of the sword. The decision was in favor of the North, so that her construction becomes the law, and should be accepted.

—*James Longstreet*

We have fought this fight as long and as well as we know how. We have been defeated. For us, as Christian people, there is now but one course to pursue. We must accept the situation.

—General Lee after Appomattox

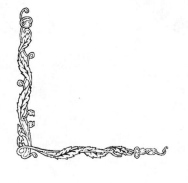
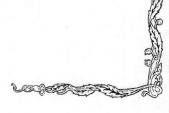

P. G. T. Beauregard

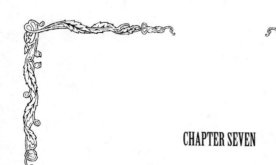

CHAPTER SEVEN

Reunion and Repatriation

After the war, Lee urged his countrymen to stop looking back. He counseled rejecting bitterness, accepting of the present and committing oneself to building a brighter tomorrow.

Bring up your children to be Americans, Lee told the fallen South. Now that the War Between the States had been fought and decided, maintaining allegiance to the Confederacy could serve no worthwhile purpose to anyone.

Lee may never have spoken words any wiser.

The thought of abandoning the country and all that must be left in it is abhorrent to my feelings, and I prefer to struggle for its restoration and share its fate rather than give up all as lost.

—General Lee's response to suggestions that he leave the country instead of live under Federal authority

True Patriotism sometimes requires of men to act exactly contrary, at one period, to that which it does at another, and the motive which impels them—the desire to do right—is precisely the same.

—*Robert E. Lee*

I have fought against the people of the North because I believed they were seeking to wrest from the South its dearest rights. But I have never cherished toward them bitter or vindictive feelings, and have never seen the day when I did not pray for them.

—*Robert E. Lee*

I did believe at the time that [war] was an unnecessary condition of affairs and might have been avoided, if forbearance and wisdom had been practiced on both sides.

—*A portion of Lee's postwar testimony to the Congressional Committee on Reconstruction*

I can only judge by the past. I cannot pretend to foresee events.

—*excerpt of Lee's testimony before the Committee on Reconstruction, February 17, 1866*

I think it is the duty of every citizen, in the present condition of the country, to do all in his power to aid in the restoration of peace and harmony, and in no way to oppose the policy of the State or general government directed to that object.

—General Lee's letter accepting the presidency of Washington College, August 24, 1865

I have led the young men of the South in battle; I have seen many of them die in the field; I shall devote my remaining energies to training young men to do their duty in life.

—*Robert E. Lee*

Madam, do not train up your children in hostility to the government of the United States. Remember, we are one country now. Dismiss from your mind all sectional feelings, and bring them up to be Americans.

—*General Lee as president of Washington College, Lexington, Virginia*

Abandon your animosities, and make your sons Americans.

—*Robert E. Lee*

Sir, if you ever again to presume to speak disrespectfully of General Grant in my presence, either you or I will sever his connection with this university.

—*General Lee speaking to a member of his board*
at Washington College, Lexington, Virginia

Go home, all you boys who fought with me, and help to build up the shattered fortunes of our old state.

—*General Lee, April 9, 1865*

Go home and take up any work that offers. Accept conditions as you find them. Consider only the present and the future. Do not cherish bitterness.

—*General Lee, speaking to soldiers and civilians alike in April 1865*

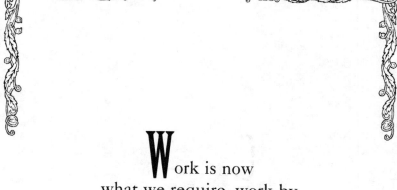

Work is now
what we require, work by
everybody. . . . By this course the
good old times of former days . . . will
return again. We may not see them
but our children will, and we will
live over again in them.

—*Robert E. Lee*

Christian faith
made him habitually
unselfish and ever willing
to sacrifice on the altar of
duty and the service
of his fellows.

—*General John Gordon speaking about
Lee after the war*

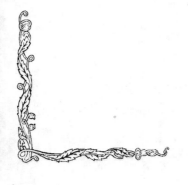

176

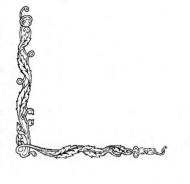

My own life has been written, but I have not looked into it. I do not wish to awaken memories of the past.

> —*General Lee, explaining that he never read a history of the Civil War or a biography of anyone who fought in it*

I'll never write my memoirs. I would be trading on the blood of my men.

> —*Robert E. Lee*